D1105259

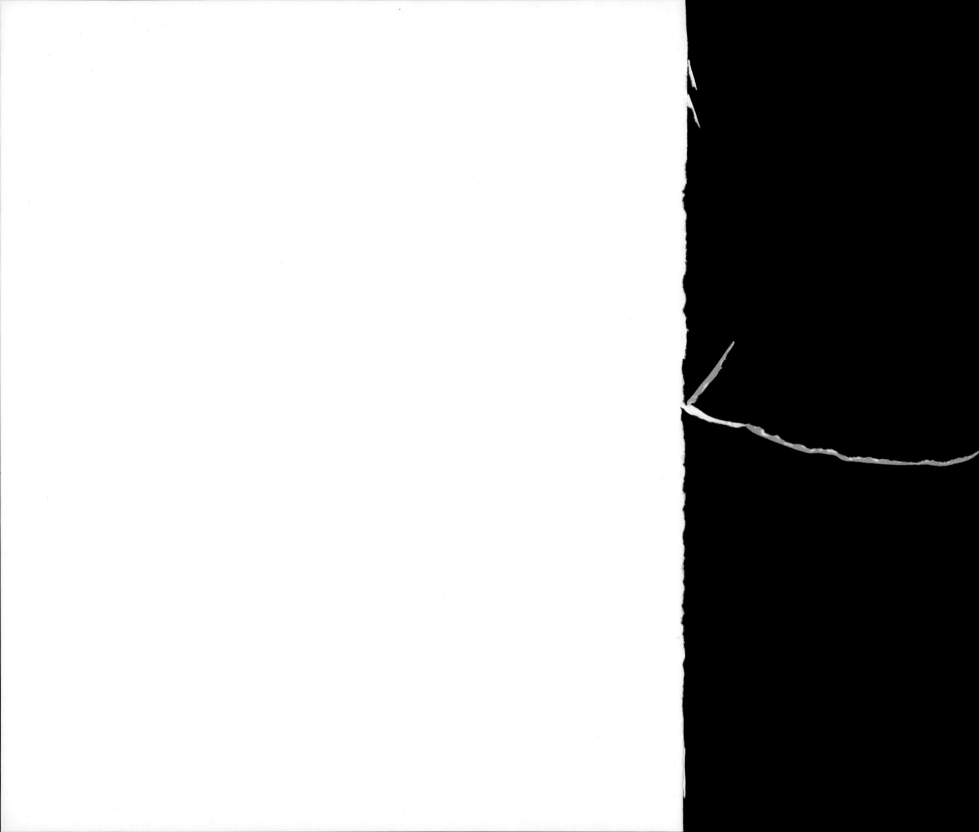

What's Congress?

Nancy Harris

Heinemann-Raintree
Chicago, Illinois

Customer Service 888-454-2279
Visit our website at **www.heinemannlibrary.com**

Designed by Kimberly R. Miracle and Betsy Wernert
Photo Research by Tracy Cummins and Heather Mauldin
Maps provided by Map Specialists
Printed in China by South China Printing Company

11 10 09 08 07
10 9 8 7 6 5 4 3 2 1

ISBN-10: 1-4034-9466-5 (hc) 1-4034-9472-X (pb)

Library of Congress Cataloging-in-Publication Data
Harris, Nancy, 1956-
  What's Congress? / Nancy Harris.
    p. cm. -- (First guide to government)
  Includes bibliographical references and index.
  ISBN-13: 978-1-4034-9466-5 (hc)
  ISBN-13: 978-1-4034-9472-6 (pb)
  1. United States. Congress--Juvenile literature. I. Title.
  JK1025.H37 2007
  328.73--dc22

2007003263

Acknowledgments
TThe author and publishers are grateful to the following for permission to reproduce copyright material: AP Photo **pp. 8** (Rogelio Solis),
14 (Gerald Herbert), **20** (Joe Marquette), **23** (Andres Leighton), **25** (Dennis Cook); Corbis **p. 10** (Wally McNamee); Getty Images
pp. 4 (Randy Wells), **6** (Chip Somodevilla), **9** (Mark Wilson), **11** (Brendan Smialowski), **15** (Mark Wilson), **16** (Diana Walker/Time
Life Pictures), **17** (Jason Connel), **19** (Mark Erickson), **26** (ROBERTO SCHMIDT/AFP), **29** (Peter Gridley); Map Resources **p. 22**;
Reuters **pp. 13** (Jason Reed), **18** (Carlos Barria), **24** (John Gress), **27** (Lee Celano), **28** (Rick Wilking).

Cover photograph reproduced with permission of A. T. Willett/Alamy.

Every effort has been made to contact copyright holders of any material reproduced in this book. Any omissions will be rectified in
subsequent printings if notice is given to the publisher.

Contents

Some words are shown in bold, **like this**. You can find out what they mean by looking in the glossary.

What Is Congress?

People in Congress work in the Capitol building.
It is in Washington, D.C.

Congress is part of the United States **federal government**. The federal government runs the whole country.

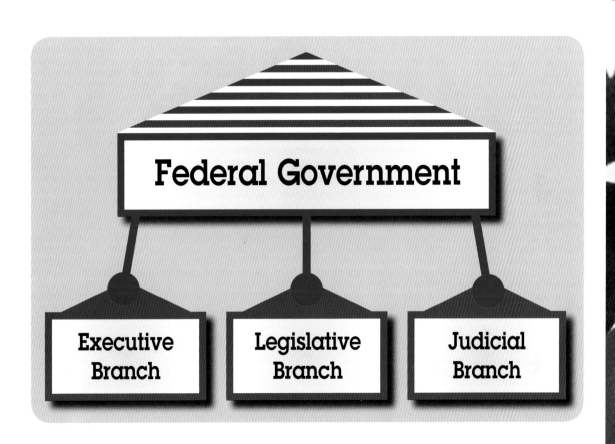

The federal government is made up of three branches (parts). Each part has a special job. One of the branches is the **legislative branch**. Congress is part of this branch.

There are two groups of people who work in Congress. They work in one of two houses: the **Senate** or the **House of Representatives**. They are called senators and representatives.

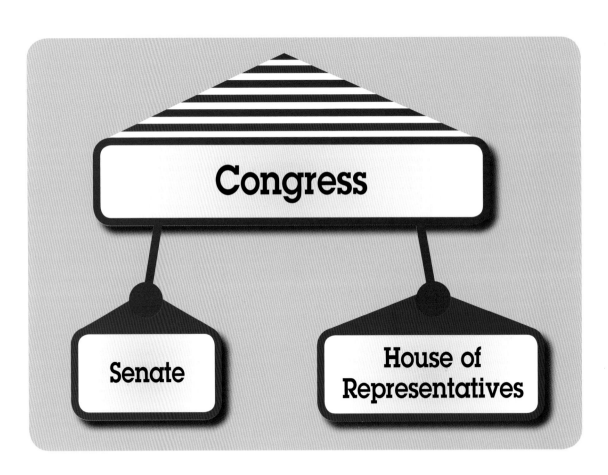

★ Senator Kennedy works in Congress.

The main job of the **legislative branch** is to make **laws**. People in Congress make laws to help people in the country.

Making Laws

It takes many steps to make a **law**. First someone has to come up with an idea for a law. The idea is then brought to Congress.

Anyone in the United States can come up with an idea for a law.

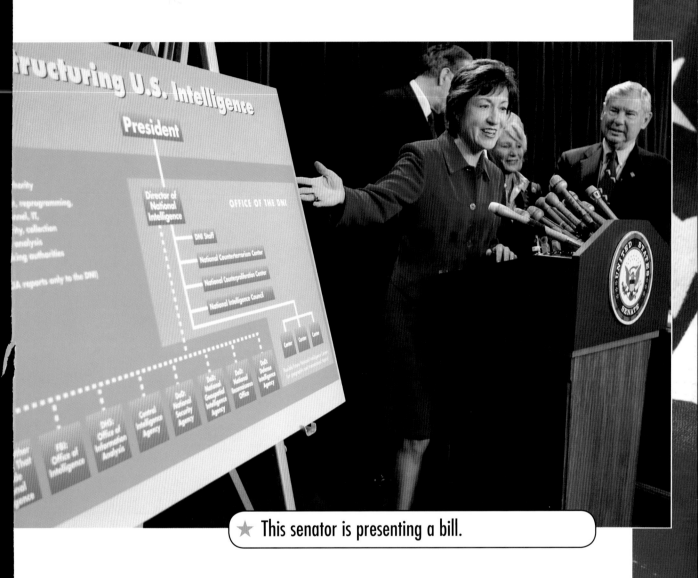

★ This senator is presenting a bill.

The idea for a law can only be brought to Congress by a senator or representative. The idea for the law is called a **bill**.

★★★ Senators meet in the Senate chambers to discuss bills and other issues.

The people in one house of Congress look at the **bill**. This can involve many meetings and discussions. Finally they **vote** to decide if the bill should become a **law**.

★ Representatives also meet to discuss bills.

If most people vote against the bill, it is no longer looked at. If most people vote in favor of the bill, it is sent to the other house of Congress.

The second house looks carefully at the bill. Then the house **votes** to decide if the **bill** should become a **law**. If most people vote in favor of the bill, it is sent to the president of the United States.

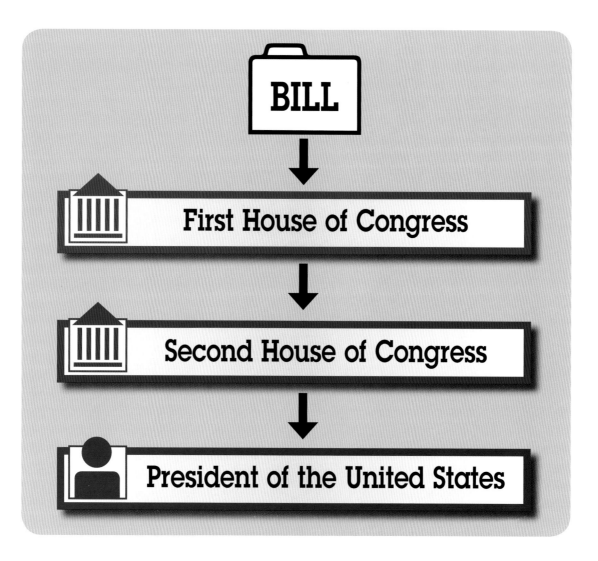

President Bush is signing a bill. It will become a new law.

If the president signs the bill, it becomes a law. The law is then **published**. It can be read by everyone in the country.

13

The Senate

Senate president

★ The Senate is also called the Upper House.

The **Senate** is made up of 100 senators. Each of the 50 states has two senators. The vice president of the United States is president of the Senate.

★ The vice president votes only if there is a tied vote.

If the Senate **votes** on a **bill** and the vote is tied, the vice president votes. The vice president does this to break the tie.

Who Can Be a Senator?

There are rules that say who can run for senator. These rules must be met before you can run for the **Senate**.

⭐ Hillary Clinton was **elected** senator of New York in 2000.

People who run for senator speak to people in their state.

The rules are:

- You must be at least 30 years old.
- You must be a United States **citizen** for nine years before your election.
- You must live in the state you are representing during the time of the election.

17

How Do You Become a Senator?

★ People vote in private booths.

Senators are **elected** by the American people. People **vote** to choose their state's senators.

They choose from a list of people running in their state. The votes are counted and the person who has the most votes wins.

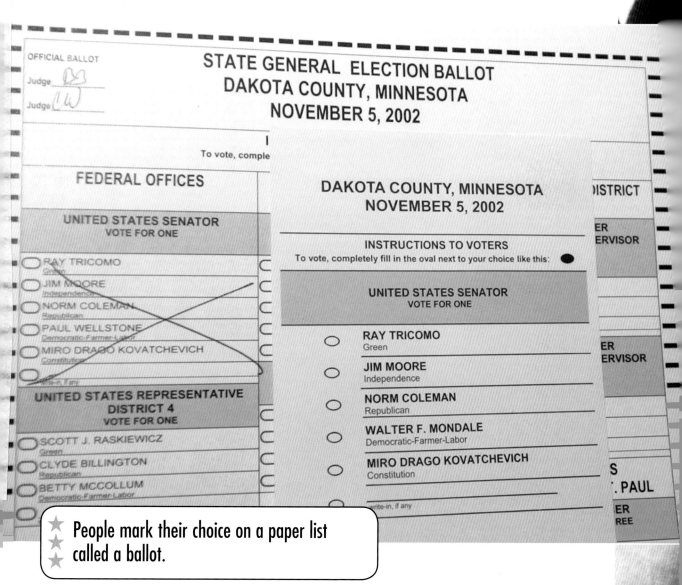

People mark their choice on a paper list called a ballot.

The House of Representatives

There are currently 435 members in the **House of Representatives**. Each state has at least one representative.

★ The House of Representatives is also called the Lower House.

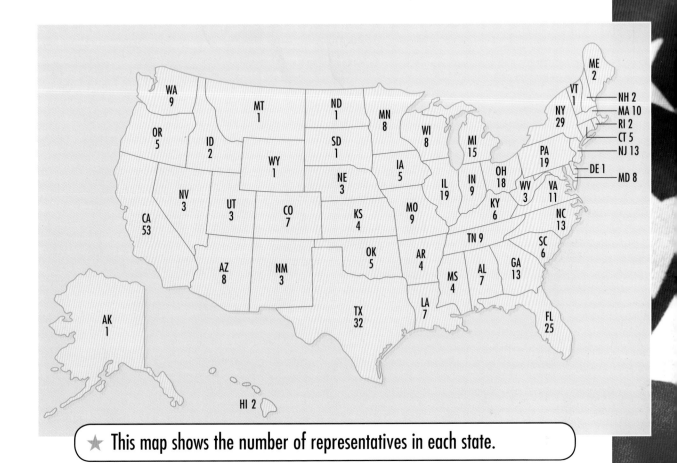

★ This map shows the number of representatives in each state.

The number of representatives a state can have is determined by how many people live in the state. States that have a lot of people have more representatives. The number of representatives changes as the population changes.

★ This map shows the four congressional districts in Arkansas.

Each representative represents people who live in a specific area of his or her state. These areas are called **congressional districts**.

The **House of Representatives** also has four **delegates** and a resident commissioner. They represent the United States territories. These are areas that are part of the United States but are not states.

Luis Fortuño represents Puerto Rico in the House of Representatives.

Who Can Be a Representative?

There are rules that say who can run for representative. These rules must be met before you can run.

★★★ Tammy Duckworth ran for representative in the state of Illinois in 2006.

★★★ Nancy Pelosi became the first female leader of the House of Representatives in 2007.

The rules are:

- You must be at least 25 years old.
- You must be a United States **citizen** for seven years before your election.
- You must live in the state you are representing during the time of the election.

How Do You Become a Representative?

Representatives are **elected** by the American people. People **vote** to choose who they want to be their representative.

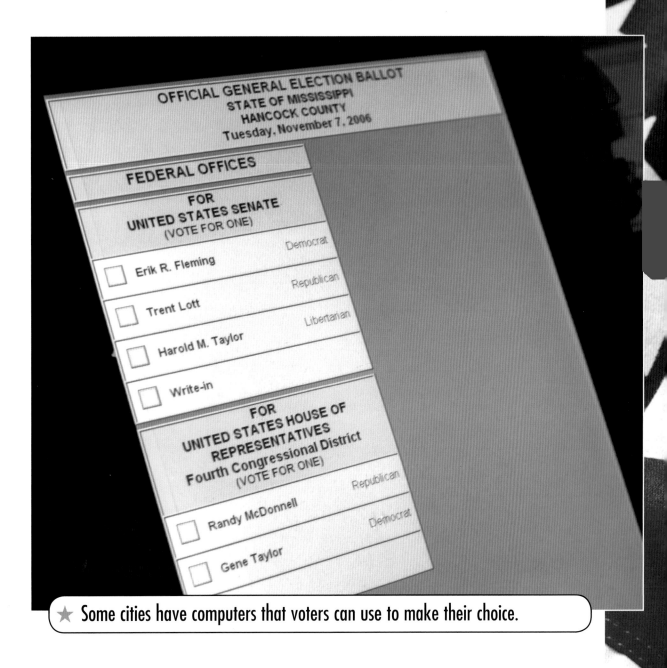

OFFICIAL GENERAL ELECTION BALLOT
STATE OF MISSISSIPPI
HANCOCK COUNTY
Tuesday, November 7, 2006

FEDERAL OFFICES

FOR
UNITED STATES SENATE
(VOTE FOR ONE)

Democrat
☐ Erik R. Fleming

Republican
☐ Trent Lott

Libertarian
☐ Harold M. Taylor

☐ Write-in

FOR
UNITED STATES HOUSE OF
REPRESENTATIVES
Fourth Congressional District
(VOTE FOR ONE)

Republican
☐ Randy McDonnell

Democrat
☐ Gene Taylor

★ Some cities have computers that voters can use to make their choice.

They choose from a list of people running in their area. The votes are counted, and the person who has the most votes wins.

How Long Can You Work in Congress?

Representatives are **elected** to serve in Congress for two years. Senators are elected to serve in Congress for six years. Senators and representatives can run for office as many times as they like.

★ Senator Kennedy has served in Congress since 1962.
He is from Massachusetts.

Congress is an important part of our government. The people in Congress represent the people of the United States. They make rules and decisions for all United States **citizens**.

Glossary

bill written proposal or idea for a new law. A law is a rule people must obey in a state or in the country.

citizen person who is born in the United States. People who have moved to the United States from another country can become citizens by taking a test.

congressional district specific area in a state. Each area has a representative in the House of Representatives.

delegate person who works in the House of Representatives and lives in one of the United States territories

elect choose a leader by voting

federal government group of leaders who run the entire country. In a federal government, the country is made up of many states.

House of Representatives house (group) in Congress where representatives from each state work. Congress is where laws are made.

law rule people must obey in a state or country

legislative branch part of the United States federal government that makes laws. Congress is the legislative branch.

publish print a text and make it available to the public

Senate house (group) in Congress where two senators from each state work. Congress is where laws are made.

vote choose who you want to be a leader

More Books to Read

An older reader can help you with these books:

Dubius, Muriel. *The U.S. House of Representatives*. Mankato, MN: Capstone Press, 2004.

Dubius, Muriel. *The U.S. Senate*. Mankato, MN: Capstone Press, 2004.

LeVert, Suzanne. *Congress*. New York: Scholastic, 2005.

Web Sites

Ben's Guide to Government (http://bensguide.gpo.gov/) gives young readers information about how the United States government works.

Kids in the House (http://clerkkids.house.gov/) is a Web site with information about the House of Representatives.

Visiting the Capitol Building

You can visit the United States Capitol building Monday through Saturday from 9 am to 4:30 pm. You must have a ticket to visit the Capitol.

The United States Capitol address is:
The United States Capitol
Capitol Hill
Washington, D.C. 20515

Index